HOW THINGS WORK

GROOVY
GADGETS

p

This is a Parragon Publishing Book
This edition published in 2001

Parragon Publishing
Queen Street House
4 Queen Street
Bath BA1 1HE, UK

ISBN 0-75255-298-8

Printed in Dubai, U.A.E

Produced by
Monkey Puzzle Media Ltd
Gissing's Farm
Fressingfield
Suffolk IP21 5SH
UK

Illustrations: Studio Liddell
Designer: Tim Mayer
Cover design: David West Children's Books
Editor: Linda Sonntag
Editorial assistance: Lynda Lines and Jenny Siklós
Indexer: Caroline Hamilton
Project manager: Katie Orchard

Photos supplied by Tony Stone Images 11 (Bruce
Ayres), 24 (Stephen Johnson), 31 (Arthur Tilley),
42 (Jon Riley), and MPM Images.

CONTENTS

CELL-PHONE

Recall and redial
Recall brings names, phone numbers, addresses, and notes from the memory and displays them on the screen. Redial calls the last number used.

On-Off buttons
The cellphone is switched on and powered up by the On button. It can receive incoming calls in this condition, but with the display light and other unnecessary circuits switched off to save battery power. When switched off, it is unable to send or receive calls, but tiny amounts of electricity still keep the memory active so it remembers its stored information.

Number (digit) buttons
These buttons are pressed to call a specific telephone number or to choose numbered options from the lists and menus on the screen.

Case
The cellphone is protected inside a strong plastic case molded to fit easily in the hand. It may have another cover over the top to cushion the phone from knocks, protect it from splashes, and reduce the risk of the phone being switched on or buttons being pressed by accident.

Mouthpiece
This is a miniature, simplified microphone, the same as in a normal telephone handset.

Hash and star buttons
The hash (#) and star (*) are used for automated calls when communicating with a recorded voice and computer, where a number button might cause confusion. For example, the hash button may be pressed to show the end of a sequence of digits such as a credit card number.

Powerpack
Rechargeable batteries give many hours of call time and more than a week of standby time (switched on and able to receive calls). They are recharged by plugging the phone into its power supply recharger which is connected to the main power supply.

MORE AND MORE CELLPHONES

No gadget in history has sold so well and advanced so fast as the cellphone. In 1998, Finland became the first country to have more cellphones than fixed phones. By the year 2000, in many countries, more people had cellphones than those who did not. Some cellphones can be linked to the Internet and have miniature screens on them for truly mobile global communications.

Earpiece
The sounds of the other person's voice come from this miniature, simplified version of a loudspeaker.

Antenna
Radio waves are sent and received by this thin rod. It can be pulled out of the case for better reception, then pushed back in for safety.

RC815

Display information
The display shows data (information) such as the telephone number you are calling, the number of an incoming call, choices and options like numbers stored in the memory, any messages left on the answer service, the strength of the radio signal, and the amount of battery power left. Numbers, letters, and symbols on the display work by liquid crystal, or LCD technology.

Backlight
The screen is backlit for easier viewing as you press the buttons to make a call. The backlight goes out a few seconds after the last button is pressed to save battery power.

Option select buttons
Lists and menus can be viewed and changed on the display by pressing these buttons.

Three-way call
The user can call and speak to one person and then call another person so that all three may talk to each other, in a three-way conference call.

Special function buttons
The function buttons carry out shortcut tasks such as calling up the list of names and phone numbers stored in the memory or checking on redial or alarm calls.

HOW CELLPHONES WORK

A cellphone is really a low-power radio transmitter and receiver. When switched on, it sends out radio signals that are detected by nearby cellular transmitter-receivers. Each of these sends and receives by radio over a local area or "cell." Several receivers may send their identity signals back to the phone. The phone then selects the most suitable receiver and establishes connection through it to the network.

The size of a cell varies, but it is usually a few miles across. Cities where more people are packed together have small cells, because each cell can cope with only a limited number of calls. Tall buildings or hills might also disrupt signals and cause dead spots.

If you use a cellphone on the move, it detects the fading signal as it moves farther away from the cell's transmitter-receiver. As soon as possible, it automatically switches to the stronger signal in the next cell along.

PERSONAL STEREO

Audio mini-cassette
The cassette is a small case of magnetic tape used for sound only (audio). It has two spools. When the tape play direction reverses, the supply spool becomes the take-up spool.

Playback head
This detects the varying pattern of magnetic patches on the tape as it slides past and converts them into a similar pattern of electrical signals for the earpieces.

Tape guide
Revolving pulleys of smooth plastic guide the tape around corners.

Play button
This large button switches on the tape play motor and works a lever that presses the pinch wheel against the motor capstan to make the tape move along.

Tape reverse switch
The direction of the tape drive motor and capstan can be reversed so that the tape slides in the opposite direction, when the supply spool becomes the take-up spool. This means you do not have to take out the cassette and turn it over to play the other side.

Tape select
Various types of tapes have different particles in the magnetic coating. For good sound quality, these are usually ferric or Fe (iron), CrO_2 (chromium dioxide), or metal (a combination of various magnetic metals).

Fast rewind button
RW (FR or REW) makes the motor turn the supply tape spool at high speed to wind back the tape.

Fast forward button
FF (FWD) makes the motor turn the take-up tape spool at high speed to wind on the tape.

Pinch wheel
The rubber pinch wheel pushes, or pinches, the tape against the motor capstan when the play button is pressed, to make the tape move along.

Earpiece
This is an in-the-ear design that fits snugly into the middle part of the ear. The two earpieces are not identical. The plastic cases are shaped differently and marked L and R for left and right ears.

Motor capstan
This metal or plastic post is part of the shaft of the electric motor. It whizzes around and makes the tape, pressed against it by the pinch wheel, move along at a constant speed—no matter how much of the tape is on the take-up spool.

Radio/tape switch
In the radio position, the electricity supply to the tape motors and playback head circuits is switched off.

CASSETTE TAPE

Mini-cassette audio tape is about one-twelfth of an inch (4 millimeters) wide and 715ft (260m) long for a playing time of 90 minutes (C90). It is made of a flexible plastic strip coated with a layer of tiny magnetic particles, and on top of this is another layer for protection and smooth running past the playback head.

INSIDE THE EAR

Headphones or earpieces work in a similar way to loudspeakers. In the 1970s, earpieces became much smaller while still giving clear, loud sounds, especially to low or bass notes. This improvement was due to new and very powerful combinations of magnetic materials, such as samarium-cobalt. There are various earpiece designs:

• In-the-ear as shown here.

• Around-the-ear with a flexible plastic loop that hooks around the back of the ear flap.

• Side-entry where the earpiece is shaped like a button but fits sideways into the ear leaving an air gap around it. This type is worn on a headband.

• Headphones can also have a headband over the top of the head. A foam-edged, cup-shaped cushion fits over the whole ear to help cut out sounds from the surroundings.

• Some headphones have fluid-filled cushions that mold themselves exactly to the shape of the person's ear and head.

Take-up spool
This does not pull the tape along. The motor capstan and pinch wheel do that. But it does rotate gently with a built-in ability to slip, to keep the tape taut as it is fed through.

Battery compartment
Two small long-life alkaline batteries give enough electrical power to play tapes for up to 10 hours, or to listen to the radio for more than 20 hours.

Radio display
The numbers on the display show the frequencies of the radio waves, that is, how many waves per second. For example a station broadcasting on 100 mHz (megaHertz) means it produces about 100 million radio waves each second.

Mini jack plug
The standard mini jack plug is rod-shaped and one-twelfth of an inch (3.5 millimeters) wide. It has three metal contact bands along its length. The tip and middle bands send electrical signals to the left and right earpieces for stereo sound. The band at the plug's base is "common" to receive the signals coming back from both earpieces.

Tuning control
Turning this knob moves the pointer, or indicator, along the radio display dial to select different radio stations, by receiving different frequencies of radio waves.

AM/FM switch
There are two radio bands, called AM (amplitude modulation) and FM (frequency modulation).

Volume control
The volume of the sounds from the earpieces is controlled by this rotating knob.

GO-PED

Handlebars
The rider holds both handlebars and turns them to steer the Go-Ped just like a bicycle.

Throttle trigger
The trigger is linked to the engine throttle by a cable. The throttle supplies more fuel and air to the engine to increase its speed and make the vehicle go faster, up to 20mph (32kph).

Engine kill
An easily-accessible switch cuts off and stops the engine in case of problems or an emergency.

Brake lever
Pulling on the lever works the front caliper brakes by a long cable, like on a bicycle.

Handlebar stem
A safety spring on the stem allows the handlebars to move down so that they are less likely to harm the rider in case of an accident. The handlebars and stem fold flat along the foot deck for carrying and storage.

SPECIAL ENGINE

The two-stroke gasoline engine is similar to those used in some power tools, and also in certain off-road or track motorcycles. In some Go-Peds, it drives the rear tire via a roller. In others, it is linked by a transmission unit that only makes the rear wheel turn as the engine gains speed and power. This allows the vehicle to stay still with the engine running.

Frame
The main frame is made of strong but lightweight metal tubing.

Front fork
The fork holds the front wheel and tire, which turn to one side or the other and steer the vehicle.

Brake
Caliper brakes make the brake blocks press against the tire to slow down the vehicle.

Wheel and tire
The tire is not air-filled (pneumatic), but solid natural rubber. It cannot take punctures, yet it still smoothes out bumps in the road.

8

PPT

Personal powered transport is a very busy field for engineers and inventors. The small vehicles use fewer raw materials and much less fuel than a car, reducing demand for natural resources and cutting pollution.

• The Go-Ped "motorized skateboard" is small, convenient, and lightweight, and can be transported easily when not in use. It carries up to almost 400lbs (180kg) so it can be used for shopping. However, it is not good on wet and slippery surfaces.

• Similar two-wheeled scooter or cycle-type designs driven by electric motors are also being developed. They carry rechargeable powerpacks of batteries that are plugged into the main electricity supply overnight.

• The mini-bubble car has three wheels like those on a tricycle and is powered by an engine. The wrap-around clear plastic bubble protects the driver from rain and danger.

UP AND AWAY

Whenever a new vehicle or craft is invented, people begin to hold races and competitions and test each other's skills. Motorcycles soon evolved into special dirt bikes on which riders negotiate mud, hills, water jumps, and logs.

Fuel tank
The tank holds the usual mixture of gasoline and two-stroke oil designed for two-stroke gasoline engines.

Foot deck
The rider stands and balances on the deck as the vehicle moves along. He or she leans slightly to the side to go around curves, but not so much as on a motorcycle because the Go-Ped's wheels are so much smaller.

Engine
The two-stroke gasoline engine drives the rear wheel directly. Whenever it is running, the rear wheel turns.

Pull start
With the rear wheel off the ground, the start cord is pulled out sharply to turn over the engine and get it going. Once the engine has been warmed up, it can be started again after being stopped by "scooting" the Go-Ped along.

Center stand
Levered onto this stand, the Go-Ped stays upright and the rear wheel is off the ground, for starting or for staying still with the engine running and the rear wheel turning.

SCUBA

Tank
Air or a special mixture of breathing gases is pumped into here. It's at a very high pressure, so a large volume becomes extremely squeezed, or compressed, into a small space.

Water pressure
The surrounding water presses on the high-pressure diaphragm to make the valve open when necessary and to keep up the intermediate pressure in the first stage regulator chamber and the air hose.

On-off valve
This tap seals, or closes, the tank so air cannot come out into the first stage regulator. It's used to turn the tank "off" when it isn't in use and also when refilling it.

First stage regulator
The first regulator reduces the very high pressure of the air in the tank to an in-between, or intermediate, pressure in the air hose, about 80-150 pounds per square inch.

Valve
The valve keeps the high-pressure air in the tank unless the pressure in the air hose drops, then it lets some air from the tank into the first stage regulator chamber and hose.

Air hose
The first stage regulator chamber leads to the flexible air hose that carries the air to the second stage regulator.

OUT OF BREATH

There are many ways of seeing the underwater world, watching fish swim, admiring the incredible variety and color of life on the coral reef, or even hunting for shipwrecks and buried treasure. Most forms of diving require some equipment. But in free diving, the diver has no gadgets, equipment, or artificial aids at all. With plenty of care, practice, and expert help on standby, some divers can stay under for more than 20 minutes or descend below 49ft (15m). But such feats are extremely specialized and very dangerous. Most people struggle to stay under for more than a minute or descend to below about 13-16ft (4–5m).

WHAT IS SCUBA?

The letters stand for Self-Contained Underwater Breathing Apparatus. It's a piece of equipment that lets you swim freely underwater for long periods of time, without having to come up for air. Before scuba gear, divers had to hold their breath, or they were attached by tubes or hoses that carried air down to them from the surface. They also had to undergo hours of special training and be physically fit and healthy. Scuba gear, after a period of training, can be used by almost anyone. It has opened up the exciting underwater world to millions of people. The early and well-known type of scuba called the aqua lung appeared in the early 1940s. It was developed by Emil Gagnan and the famous French diver, filmmaker, writer, conservationist, and ocean expert Jacques-Yves Cousteau.

Depth gauge
The depth gauge contains a pressure sensor so the divers know how deep they are. Most divers are advised not to go below about 131ft (40m). The water pressure increases with depth, and by this depth, it becomes dangerous. When the divers return to the surface, the release of pressure on the body may cause the dangerous, even deadly condition called "the bends."

Ambient-pressure diaphragm
As the diver breathes in, the air pressure in the second stage regulator chamber falls. The outside water pressure pushes on the flexible diaphragm which curves, or bows, in, and works a lever to open the valve and let in intermediate air from the air hose.

Second stage regulator
This device lowers the intermediate pressure of the air in the air hose, to the ambient pressure in the second stage regulator chamber. The ambient pressure is the pressure of the surroundings the diver happens to be in—that is, the water pressure all around. The regulator self-adjusts so that as the diver goes down and the water pressure on the body increases, the pressure of the breathed-in air also increases. This ensures the pressures are balanced and the diver's chest can expand against the surrounding water pressure, so breathing is comfortable.

Exhaust
Breathed out air leaves the mouthpiece by pushing open flaplike valves into the exhaust manifolds, and then out into the water. It produces a stream of bubbles with each breath.

Mouthpiece
Air flows from the second stage regulator chamber through the mouthpiece, into the diver's mouth, and own breathing system.

Valve
The valve opens when worked by the ambient-pressure diaphragm and lever, to let air from the air hose pass into the second stage regulator chamber. This air can then be breathed in.

DEPTH INT TIME   MAX DEPTH   SURFACE TIME
56 MIN   198 FT   3 HR
0 58 MIN   NORMAL CONDITION

SATELLITE TV

Dish
The dish is an antenna that receives radio signals from the satellite broadcast. It must be pointed at exactly the right angle, both sideways and up, to receive the strongest signals from the satellite. Satellites that broadcast TV programs are in a special geostationary orbit (GSO) above the Equator of the Earth. So, in the northern parts of the world, satellite dishes always point south, and in the south, they point north.

Parabolic mesh
The shape of the dish and its mesh is a parabola, or similar curve. This reflects the radio signals and focuses, or concentrates, them onto the receiver.

TOO MANY DISHES
Some people complain that satellite dishes are ugly to look at. Local laws often prevent them from being attached to historic buildings.

Receiver arm
The arm holds the receiver unit at precisely the correct distance and angle from the dish to receive the focused signals.

Offset receiver
Radio signals are detected and turned into electrical signals by the receiver. This is offset, or not in line, with the center of the dish, so it does not get in the way of the incoming radio signals.

SATELLITE, TERRESTRIAL, AND CABLE
Signals for television programs can arrive at a TV set in one of three main ways.

• Satellite: This is DBS (direct broadcast by satellite). The signals are in the form of invisible radio waves that come from a satellite high up in space. They are broadcast over a wide area, and the individual dishes pick them up. As domestic dishes are small, the satellite must send out powerful signals. The main area where the signals can be received is called the satellite's "footprint."

• Terrestrial: The radio signals are beamed out by antennae on tall towers or high buildings. They can usually be received by an antenna shaped like a long bar with cross-pieces.

• Cable: The signals are sent as coded pulses of laser light flashing along a fiber-optic cable buried underground. This system is often combined with telephone and computer lines that work in the same way.

Sockets and connectors
The rear of the satellite box or unit has connections for the antenna wire, TV set, telephone line, and other equipment. It may also be linked to a computer network.

Antenna wire
The antenna wire conveys the electrical signals from the receiver into the satellite "box," or decoder. It is routed to avoid electrical equipment such as fluorescent lights that might interfere with the signals.

Remote control handset
The handset has all the buttons and controls for the decoder unit. It communicates with the decoder unit using an invisible beam, usually a low-power infra-red (weak heat) beam.

Satellite box
The "box" is basically a decoder unit. The signals coming in are in encrypted, or coded, form. You must pay for a card that allows the unit to decode the signals for viewing on a TV set.

Power unit shield
A metal case around the power unit prevents it from interfering with the delicate circuits in the rest of the decoder unit.

Controls
Some of the most important controls are duplicated on the unit itself in case the remote control unit is lost or broken.

TV guide
All the programs on all the available channels allowed by the card are displayed on the screen. This can take time, since some satellite systems have more than 100 channels.

Card reader
The card slots into a card reader that detects the magnetic codes in the card's stripes.

Decryption
The signals coming in from the satellite broadcast are encrypted, or "scrambled." The method of encryption changes regularly. Only if the card is suited for the date and channel, will the decryption unit un-scramble, or decode, the signals so they can be fed into the TV set.

Interactive TV
Some decoder units are interactive—that is they can send as well as receive. The user receives information via the satellite broadcast, for example, from a shopping channel. He or she then uses the handset to send information from the unit via a connection to the phone line, to order goods.

Smart card
The card has various code numbers represented by tiny patches of magnetism in its stripes. These include the dates and channels that have been paid for. They are matched to the broadcast information coming in with the pictures and sound. If the card is out of date or the channel is not on the accepted list, the unit stops its signals.

CAMCORDER

Zoom lens system
There are many lenses in groups along this lens system. Zooming means they move in and out to change the field or area of view. Zooming in is like looking through a telescope—it shows a small area greatly enlarged. Zooming out shows a broader view at less magnification, so the scene looks farther away.

Objective
The large lenses at the front are called the objective because they point at the object—the item or scene that is being recorded. They gather light rays from the scene and begin to bend or focus them as they pass through the lens system inside the camera.

Zoom return
A spring on a sliding rod makes sure that the lens system slides smoothly for zooming in and out.

Zoom gearing
This moves the main lens system forward and backward to zoom the image in and out.

Microphone
Two small microphones angled to each side behind the protective grill detect stereo sound, which is recorded on the tape.

Screen backlight
This switches on the backlight for the screen so that it can be viewed in low-light conditions. It can be switched off in bright conditions to save power, when the LCD screen works by reflected light.

Focus
The focus knob moves the lenses in relation to each other to make the picture clear and sharp.

Video tape
The electronic signals from the CCD circuits (representing the picture) and microphones (the sound) are recorded on a video tape in the same way as a VCR. In some designs, the cassette is removed. In others, the camcorder is plugged into a VCR later to transfer the recording.

CCD
The charge coupled device (CCD) is like a miniature screen that senses light rays and turns their positions and brightness into patterns of digital electronic signals.

Powerpack
A pack of rechargeable batteries provides power for the motors of the tape recorder and lens movements, and for the electronic circuits and display screen.

Eyepiece
The user looks through this to see the viewfinder, which shows the pictures that the camcorder is taking.

Viewfinder
Unlike the photographic camera, light rays don't come all the way through the camcorder, so the user cannot see the scene. Instead, a miniature TV screen in the viewfinder shows the user what is being filmed.

video Hi8
steady shot
XR

CAMERA-RECORDER
A camcorder is a combination of a video camera and video recorder. The video camera is designed to take many still pictures or images (usually 25) each second. When they are played back, they give the impression of continuous movement as on a TV screen. There is no photographic film in a camcorder like there is in a movie camera. The patterns of light rays that form the images are converted into corresponding patterns of electronic signals by components called CCDs—charge coupled devices. The signals are then recorded as tiny patches of magnetism onto a video tape.

Display screen
Pictures recorded on the tape can be played back for several viewers on the LCD screen. They can either be saved, or stored for later use to save tape time, or erased and recorded over if they are not wanted.

THE SHRINKING CAMCORDER
Early camcorders were so heavy that they had to be held steady with two hands. They were complicated to use and worked only in bright light. Today's versions fit into the palm of the hand. They have simple controls with auto-focus and auto-exposure to adjust the camcorder to suit the changing brightness of the light. They work even in light levels that are almost too dim for the human eye.

VR HEADSET

Headset
The computer sends electrical signals to the headset screens which convert these into light rays. The user sees the patterns of rays with his or her eyes and understands them as a scene in his or her brain.

3-D vision
In the vision centers at the back of the user's brain, the two slightly different views from the two eyes are merged to give a single view in the "mind's eye." This has width, height, and also depth, or the illusion of distance. It is 3-D stereoscopic vision.

Video controls
These knobs control the screen color, brightness, and contrast, like on a normal TV set.

Speaker
A speaker plays sounds directly into the ear on that side. Some headsets have earpieces or built-in headphones, which help to cut out unwanted sounds from around the user.

Strap adjuster
The straps are adjusted to fit the head size and shape of the individual user.

PCB
The main electronic components are fitted into a PCB, printed circuit board. This is made with metal strips already built or "printed" into it. The components are then fitted onto the board so that the metal strips act as wires to connect them.

Topstrap
A wide strap passes over the top of the head to join the backstrap at the back, so that the headset is comfortable.

Screens
The screens show the images for the eyes. They show slightly different images for each eye. In real life, the two eyes see slightly different views since they look at the scene from slightly different places and directions.

Audio controls
The audio knobs control the volume of the stereo sound, its balance (whether it is too loud in the left or right ear), and its tone of high and low notes.

SERIOUS VR

VR systems vary from simple slip-on headsets to full helmets and body suits that look like deep-sea diving suits. These not only provide sight and sound, but also physical pressure for the skin's sense of touch, and possibly even scents for the nose. They also have feedback. They detect the user's movements, so that the computer can alter what he or she sees, hears, and feels. The user seems to be moving around in a complete virtual world.

VR can be a lot of fun for flying airplanes, shooting aliens, and playing other games. But it also has many serious uses. It helps to train people such as pilots, surgeons, firefighters, and rescue workers, where a mistake in the virtual world harms no one.

TAKING OFF TO NOWHERE

A form of VR has been used for many years in flight simulators where pilots train. The simulator is a whole room, and the computer controls large motors or pistons that make it tilt and rock like a real aircraft.

UR sensory glove
The glove is an input device. It gathers information, turns it into electrical signals, and feeds them into the UR computer for analysis and processing. In this case, the information is about the detailed ways the hand and fingers flex and move to push, pull, grasp, grip, and make other actions. Then, when the computer shows a hand moving on its screens, it can use the data from the glove to make these movements more realistic.

Sensor wires
Thin, flexible wires carrying small amounts of electricity are built into the glove. As the wires stretch or bend, they alter the amount of electricity passing through them. The computer detects these changes and can then work out how the fingers are moving.

Finger rings
The rings gather information about the hand's finger movements and gripping pressure.

WHAT IS VIRTUAL REALITY?

It's an object or scene that seems real to the senses of sight, hearing, touch, and smell, but is not. It is virtual, or unreal. It exists only as electronic signals in a computer, as spots of light on a screen, and sound waves from an earpiece. A central computer processes all the information and sends out the signals to various pieces of equipment. These give us the illusion of seeing, hearing, touching, and even smelling— so we get a sense of reality.

CD PLAYER

Reflection
A micro-pit on the CD scatters the light that shines up from the laser beam below. The shiny metal between the micro-pits does reflect the beam, which travels back down again.

Focusing lens
This lens focuses the laser beam onto a tiny spot on the disc.

Reflected laser beam
The reflected laser beam passes down the optical tube toward the light sensors.

Semi-silvered mirror
The laser beam from the laser is reflected up here toward the disc. If the beam is reflected by a shiny flat metal portion between the micro-pits, it passes back down through this mirror to the light sensors below.

Optical tube
This contains the mirrors, lenses, and sensors for the laser beam. It slides along as the screw thread turns to read different parts of the disc.

Cylindrical lens
A lens makes the reflected laser beam narrower, or more focused, before it shines on the light sensors.

STORING INFORMATION
Since its introduction onto the open market in the early 1980s, the CD has proved itself as a small, light, tough, convenient way to store information. An audio CD can store up to 75 minutes of high-quality sound or over 100 million words of text. A CD-ROM (read-only memory) for a computer or similar machine holds about 640 MB (megabytes) of data, programs, and other information. Blank CDs are inexpensive and can have the pits "burned" or "toasted" into them by a CD burner. They are used for storing computer information.

Light sensors
A pad of sensors produces a tiny pulse of electricity when illuminated by the reflected laser beam. This is an "on" or 1 signal of the digital code. A micro-pit on the disc means no reflection, which gives an "off" or 0 signal.

Compact disc
The disc is made mainly of plastic and is 5in (12cm) across. The working part is its underside, which is coated with a thin layer of shiny aluminum-based metal.

CD drive motor
Under the CD is a variable speed motor that makes the disc spin around. A vinyl record spins at a constant speed, such as 33.3 turns, or revolutions, per minute (rpm) for a long player (LP). The CD turns at a varying speed according to whether the inside or outside part of the track is being read, so that the pits and flats always pass the laser beam at a constant rate.

CD track (underside)
As on a vinyl record, the CD track spirals out from the center, around and around toward the edge. It is more than 3mi (5km) long and contains more than 3 billion micro-pits. The sequence of micro-pits is a code for information.

Micro-pits (underside)
The micro-pits are microscopic holes, or gaps, in the CD track. The pits and the flat areas between them are read at the rate of 1.3 million per second.

Semiconductor laser
A small solid-state laser produces the reddish-colored laser beam for reading the sequences of micro-pits on the disc.

Ribbon connector
These flexible multi-wire connectors are used to link parts which move in relation to each other, such as the optical tube and the main circuit board in this CD player.

Optical drive screw
A screw thread turned by an electric motor moves the whole optical tube so that it follows the spiraling track of micro-pits as the disc spins. Unlike a vinyl record, the CD starts playing nearest the middle and finishes out at the edge.

DIGITAL AND ANALOG

The CD is digital. This means it stores information as a sequence, or code, of numbers or digits. In fact, it has only two digits, 0 and 1. The 0 can be thought of as no reflection from the disc where there is a micro-pit. The 1 is a reflection where there isn't a micro-pit. Using two numbers is called binary code. Computers work using binary code, too, making CDs very useful for them.

Analog systems do not use numbers or on-offs. They use continually varying quantities like a "wave" of electrical voltage. Although the wave is supposed to vary, much smaller natural variations occur within it and mean that it is not an exact way to carry information. Because it is played or copied many times, the variations and errors can build up. Copying digital information means copying out lists of 0s and 1s, which is not prone to errors.

WIDESCREEN TV

Stereo sound
Two sets of loudspeakers play different sounds for the left and right channels. These reach our left and right ears and give the effect of sounds spread out in front of us across the breadth of the screen. This is known as stereophonic sound.

Wide sound
Extra loudspeakers positioned to the sides or back help to spread out the sound. Sometimes a car or plane can be heard approaching from the side before it appears on the screen.

Subsound
A large loudspeaker built into the TV cabinet produces very deep notes. These are not so much heard as felt—for example, the shudder of an earthquake or the rumbling of thunder.

Zoom control
The size and proportions of the picture on the screen can be changed with the zoom control.

Stand
The widescreen TV is very heavy. It has a strong, stable cabinet as a stand. This also stores a VCR and its videotape cassettes, a DVD player and its discs, and maybe the week's television broadcast guide.

Pixels

A pixel, or picture, element is a tiny unit of the screen whose brightness and color can be controlled. It consists of tiny dots that glow in different colors—red, green, and blue. Pixels are built up like spots of color in a mosaic to make the whole screen picture.

Picture quality

The quality of a TV picture depends on many features such as the quality of the original electrical signals and the number of lines on the screen. Standard TV screens have pictures made up of some 100,000 pixels arranged in 625 horizontal lines across the screen. The lines are scanned, or made to glow, from top to bottom.

TU SCREEN PROPORTIONS

The proportion, or ratio, of the screen is the length from side to side compared with the height from top to bottom. A typical TV is about 4:3, that is, one-third again as wide as it is high. However, a full-sized movie screen in a cinema has the ratio 16:9, almost twice as wide as it is high. This was designed to fit comfortably into our field of vision, or view, which is the area in front of us that our eyes can see and take in easily. It allows us to watch much broader, more spectacular scenes. Widescreen TV has similar proportions to a movie screen for the same spectacular effect.

HDTV

Picture quality improves with HD (high definition) TV. The screen has more and closer-together horizontal lines, over 1,000, compared to the normal 625.

Wide screen

The screen is much wider than that of a conventional TV screen. Its proportions suit the natural field of view of our eyes better.

Words on-screen

Some countries have Teletext, which may have over 1,000 pages of writing giving all kinds of information such as news headlines, sports scores, weather forecasts, and ads for vacations, money loans, and many other items.

TU SCREEN SIZES

The size of a TV, or monitor, screen is usually measured diagonally, from one top corner to the bottom opposite corner. However, the edges of the screen may be covered by the frame of the plastic case for the set so the amount of screen that actually shows the picture is slightly less. A typical small "portable" TV screen is 14in (35cm). A standard domestic TV may be 25in (63cm). A widescreen TV may be 40in (100cm) or more. The screen is the front of a glass part called a "tube" (CRT, cathode ray tube, or vacuum tube). It looks like a mushroom lying on its side with the "stalk" projecting backward. FST is a flatter, squarer tube. The screen surface is flat instead of slightly domed and has more angular instead of rounded corners.

VCR/DVD

If there are no suitable programs on terrestrial, satellite, or cable TV, the VCR (video cassette recorder-player) and DVD (digital versatile disk player) can show pre-recorded programs.

21

PERSONAL COMPUTER (PC)

Computer tower
Most of the computer's circuits and drives are housed in a tower unit. This can be placed on a shelf or nearby table if there is not enough room on the desktop.

Hard disk drive
The hard disk is really a stack of magnetic disks in a case. It is kept in the computer and holds all the computer's programs and data.

Magnetic disk drive
Removable disks can be placed in this drive. Information is fed from the computer, or written, onto the disk and recorded as tiny patches of magnetism on the disk surface. Later, the information may be read, or fed back into the computer. This means the disks are read-write instead of read-only.

Motherboard
The large printed circuit board contains most of the main microchips and components. They include the CPU (central processing unit) which is the computer's "central brain," and the RAM (random access memory chips) which acts as its working memory.

Optical disc drive
Compact discs (CDs) are placed in this drive. They store information as patterns of microscopic pits on their surface and are read optically by laser light. Many computers have read-only optical drives. This means the information stored on them can only be taken from the disc into the computer. New information cannot be taken from the computer and stored on the disc. So the drive and discs are called CD-ROM, compact disc read-only memory.

Rear panel
On panels at the back of the computer, there are sockets and connectors to link it by wires and cables to the monitor screen, keyboard, mouse, and extra devices, or peripherals.

Loudspeaker
The computer may be able to play music from its discs or programs. It also makes various beeps, pings, and other sounds. These show that it is working correctly, has completed a task, or cannot carry out a process.

Mouse
Moving the mouse moves a pointer or cursor on the screen onto various choices, options, lists, and menus. Clicking a button on the mouse selects that option. In image-based programs, the mouse can be used like a pen to draw and change pictures.

High capacity magnetic drive
Larger magnetic disks that hold more information are slotted in here.

Mouse mat
This gives a flat surface for the mouse to roll on. A rubber ball inside the mouse must roll for the mouse to work.

ADD-ONS

A basic computer usually has a main unit with the circuits and drives, a keyboard, a mouse, and a monitor. The main unit and monitor may be in the same case. But there are dozens of add-ons, plug-ins, or peripherals that can be connected to the computer. A common one is the printer to produce "hard copy"—writing or pictures on paper instead of on the screen. Others that input or send signals to the computer include an image scanner, microphone, digital camera, joystick, and music keyboard. Then there are outputs, which receive signals from the computer. These include a hi-fi system, a large and accurate printer called a plotter, image projector, and moving robot arm.

Monitor
The monitor works in the same way as the screen of a TV set. But the circuits that receive the signals are not the same. The signals coming from a computer are very different from the signals coming from a TV antenna.

Screen base
The screen can be swiveled and tilted on its base for the best view, and to reduce eyestrain and neckache.

Alphanumeric keys
The letters of the alphabet from A–Z, and the standard numerals from 0 –9 are on this area of the keyboard, laid out in the same way as on the traditional typewriter.

Special function keys
Usually labeled F1, F2, and so on, these are "shortcut" keys that have special jobs according to the program being used. For example, one of them may bring up a particular list or menu of options such as the colors for words.

Numeric function keys
As well as being used simply for numbers, these keys can be given special jobs, like moving the cursor or pointer up one paragraph in a written document.

COMPUTER TERMINALS

The computer shown here is a complete working unit and can be used on its own. A computer terminal may look similar. But it is usually just a monitor, keyboard, and mouse. These are connected by longer wires or a network to a main computer. Many other terminals are connected, too. Lots of people can use the same computer at the same time, sharing the information and programs.

VIDEOPHONE

LCD
The small screen does not use a "tube" like a normal television set. It has a much flatter, lighter liquid crystal display (LCD).

Flip-up screen
The screen is lit and activated by tilting or lifting it up at an angle. This also switches on the videophone's camera.

Earpiece
This works in the opposite way from the mouthpiece. It receives electrical signals along its wire and converts them into sound waves that you can hear.

Loudspeaker
The loudspeaker produces the sound of the other person's voice if the handset is not being used. It has to give out only a limited range of sound pitches or frequencies, those produced by the voice, compared to the music of a full orchestra. So it can be small and simple compared to a music system loudspeaker.

Digital display
Telephone numbers and other information are displayed here.

Telephone handset
This works in the same way as the normal telephone handset, so you can speak to and hear the person at the other end of the line.

Mouthpiece
The mouthpiece is a simple microphone that picks up the sound waves from your voice and converts them into patterns of electrical signals. This is the opposite of the earpiece. The signals go along wires in the curly cord into the videophone.

LCD TECHNOLOGY
A liquid crystal display (LCD) is much smaller, flatter, and lighter than the "tube" for a normal television screen. However, its picture isn't quite as sharp and clear. In an LCD, tiny spots of colored crystalline substances, like colored Jello, let through or stop light by a certain amount according to how much electricity is passed through them. In the backlit LCD display, the light comes from the lowest, or base layer, of the screen behind the crystals, passes through them, and shines into the eyes. This is brighter than the non-backlit version, where light from the surroundings is reflected off the back of the screen. Most digital watches have non-backlit LCD displays. Backlit LCDs are used in laptop and palmtop computers, in miniature and wristwatch TVs, and in some giant screens at sports stadiums, music concerts, and similar big events.

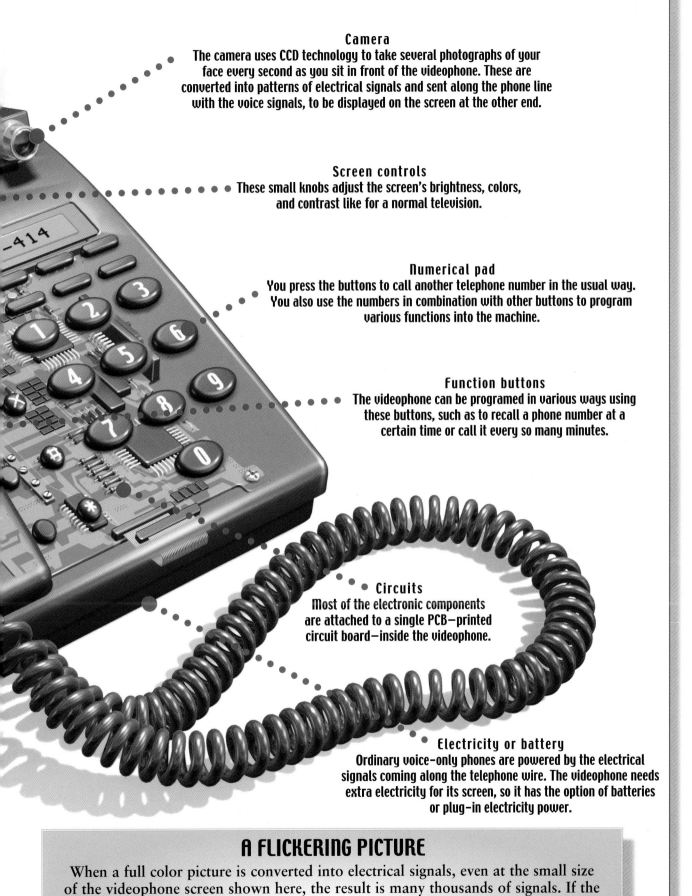

Camera
The camera uses CCD technology to take several photographs of your face every second as you sit in front of the videophone. These are converted into patterns of electrical signals and sent along the phone line with the voice signals, to be displayed on the screen at the other end.

Screen controls
These small knobs adjust the screen's brightness, colors, and contrast like for a normal television.

Numerical pad
You press the buttons to call another telephone number in the usual way. You also use the numbers in combination with other buttons to program various functions into the machine.

Function buttons
The videophone can be programed in various ways using these buttons, such as to recall a phone number at a certain time or call it every so many minutes.

Circuits
Most of the electronic components are attached to a single PCB—printed circuit board—inside the videophone.

Electricity or battery
Ordinary voice-only phones are powered by the electrical signals coming along the telephone wire. The videophone needs extra electricity for its screen, so it has the option of batteries or plug-in electricity power.

A FLICKERING PICTURE

When a full color picture is converted into electrical signals, even at the small size of the videophone screen shown here, the result is many thousands of signals. If the picture is designed to show movement, this becomes millions of signals per second. Most phone lines are unable to carry this much information. They are designed for the relatively limited number of signals representing the sound of the voice. Because of this limited capacity, only a small color picture can be sent and this can change only a few times a second, producing a jumping or flickering image.

MEDICAL SCANNER

Rotating drum
The drum inside the casing twists so that the magnets and detectors can rotate around the body and scan it from different angles.

Superconducting magnets
Very powerful magnets "magnetize" the body for a short period and affect the way the billions of hydrogen atoms in its parts and tissues line up and spin around. (Hydrogen, H, is one of the most common chemical elements in the body, making up part of each water molecule, H_2O—and the body is almost two-thirds water).

Patient
The patient lies still on a bedlike table. She or he may be given a sedative to relax the body and mind and calm any worries. A particular substance or chemical may also be injected into the patient to make certain kinds of scan clearer.

Scanner casing
The working parts of the scanner are contained inside a strong metal case, to protect the people on the outside and the delicate circuits and components inside.

Sliding table
The table slides to move the patient along so that successive horizontal levels or sections of the body can be scanned, one at a time. This builds up a 3-D image.

Connecting cables
Thick cables containing many individual wires link the scanner and control console.

A WORRYING EXPERIENCE

Having a scan can be a worrying process. But it is painless and usually over very quickly. Modern scanning machines are made to be as harmless as possible, and there are virtually no risks in using them.

Radio units
Radio waves are beamed through the magnetized body and affect the way the hydrogen atoms line up and spin. As they alter their alignment and spin, the atoms send out their own tiny pulses of radio waves, which are detected by the radio sensors. They form electrical signals, which are sent to the computer along with signals about the angle, strength, and timing of the beams.

Monitor screen
The scan images are shown on the TV-style computer monitors. Different body parts such as nerves, bones, and blood have different amounts of brightness or intensity. These can be color-coded by the computer to make the differences clearer.

Protective screen
A protective wall surrounds the operators and other people and shields them from any harmful effects of the scanning equipment. For an individual patient who is in the room for a short time the risks are almost zero. But they increase for the operators and other staff who are there hour after hour, week after week.

Viewing window
Operators can watch through the window to make sure that the patient is alright and the equipment is working properly. The glass is specially strengthened and treated for protection.

Computer
A huge amount of computer power is needed to decode the signals coming in from the radio sensors and other equipment, analyze them, and gradually build up the scan pictures section by section.

Controls
The operator controls the computer, which controls the scanner and other equipment. Most of the instructions are fed in by typing them in with a keyboard as with a normal computer.

Operator
The operator is highly skilled in various areas including medicine, human anatomy (body structure), computer operations, and engineering.

KINDS OF MEDICAL IMAGING

There are many ways of looking inside the body without cutting it open:

- X rays are useful for showing bones and teeth. Modern X rays are very safe but strong X rays can harm the body.

- CT (computerized tomography, or CAT—computerized axial tomography) uses weak X rays that are not harmful. It scans the body slice by slice, and puts the slices together for a detailed 3-D result.

- An ultrasound scan beams sound waves, too high-pitched for our hearing, into the body and analyzes the echoes. It is used to examine babies in the womb.

- The MR (magnetic resonance imaging) scan gets detailed results by putting the body in a powerful magnetic field and beaming radio waves through it.

- PET (positron emission tomography) involves injecting "tagged" substances into the body, such as hormones or blood sugar. The scanner tracks the substance and shows how it is used. PET scans are often used on the brain.

INTERNET

LOGGING ONTO THE NET

The Internet is the worldwide international network of interlinked computers and other electronic devices. It is not really one single network but complex groups of smaller networks joined together. You need a computer that plugs into the phone line or telecom system to use it. You "log on" by sending signals to your ISP, Internet service provider. The ISP's own computer acts as a go-between, or intermediate, between your computer and the whole network. You "download" by receiving along the phone line the electrical signals that represent various forms of information such as words, pictures, sounds, and computer programs, and storing these in your computer.

Global telecom network
The telecommunications network involves telephone exchanges, computers of all shapes and sizes, fax machines, land lines, microwave and satellite links, and many other parts.

E-mail
E-mail does not use paper. You type or make a message on your computer, address it to the recipient, and send it along the telephone line to your e-mail provider. The message waits there, stored on what is basically a huge computer disk, until the recipient uses his or her computer to call up and get it.

Modem link
The modem is a device that changes the tiny digital electronic pulses inside the computer into electrical signals suitable for feeding into the telecom network.

Backward-Forward
Clicking on these arrows goes to the previous page you were looking at on the screen, or to the next page on the list.

Address
The address is not a physical place like a house or office. It is an electronic label for a certain website or e-mail recipient—more like the address of their computer.

Option panels or buttons
You can choose what to see next by using the mouse to position the computer's cursor or arrow on one of these panels, or "screen buttons," and then clicking the mouse.

Mouse

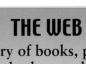

THE WEB

Imagine a vast library of books, pictures, movies, ads, music, catalogs, and other works and publications. The World Wide Web is like this but in electronic form. It exists as tiny electrical signals inside computers and whizing along telephone lines. You can look up a website, which is like taking a library book or catalog off the shelf. This is usually made by one company or organization and it is about a certain subject. You can look at the different pages on screen just as you would flick through the book. But using the Web is much quicker than visiting a library. Web sites can be continents away. They can be changed and updated at any time. Unlike a book, they are two-way—you can send information, messages, orders, and money to them as well as receiving goods or information from them.

Destination computer
The message from your computer can reach another computer on the opposite side of the world in just one second. However, the various delays and changes as it passes through the system mean that the transfer time is usually slightly longer.

Search engine
You can search the Net using a search engine. This is a computer program or application that scans the network for the key words or phrases that you enter, and shows you a list of possible addresses that might be helpful. You can search in a certain country, continent, or across the whole world.

Hub
A hub is a concentrated center where many big computers send and receive information rapidly. Gateway computers change information or data into the different forms and codes, called protocols, used in various countries.

ISP or Server

Screen and page
A page may be more than just what you can see on your screen. You may have to move or scroll the page sideways or down so you can see the rest of it as it comes onto the screen. It's like moving the large page of a newspaper or magazine around behind a smaller opening, which is the screen.

Image
Pictures tend to download (arrive in your computer) more slowly than words. They can be copied into the memory of your own computer, but they take up much more memory space than words.

Text
Words usually download very quickly. You can highlight, or choose, them, copy them into your own computer's memory, and store them in one of your own files or documents.

User's computer

SATELLITE NAVIGATION SYSTEM

Comsat
A communications satellite is part of the worldwide telecom network. It receives and sends on radio signals for telephone calls, TV programs, computer messages, and many other forms of long-distance communication.

Dish antenna
The large dish can send and receive faint or far-away signals. It can be moved by electric motors and pointed very precisely at a certain satellite, and moved to link with other satellites at different times.

Ground station
This is in communication with many satellites via its large dish and other antennas. It also contacts other stations on the ground by radio and microwave links, and by the cables and land lines of the telecom network.

Ship-to-shore
Direct radio links between a ship and land can only be carried out over limited distances. If a ship is too far away, the curve of the Earth's surface gets in the way, since most radio signals go in straight lines and not around bends. This is why satellites are so useful. They can receive signals on the uplink and then beam them down somewhere else a continent away. They act like relay or passing-on radio sets on incredibly tall towers.

Satellite orbit
A satellite has forward motion, which means that it tries to go in a straight line. It would fly off into space if it weren't for the Earth's gravity pulling it down. However, the satellite is pulled down at a rate that matches the way the Earth's surface curves around beneath. So the satellite endlessly falls to Earth, but never gets there, because the Earth endlessly curves away from it.

THE SPEED OF LIGHT

Radio and microwave signals go up and down to satellites at the fastest possible speed— the speed of light. This is about 186,000 miles per second (300,000 kilometers per second). However, some satellites are so far away that signals take more than one-tenth of a second to get there. If the signals go up and down to several satellites on their journey around the globe, the delay can add up to almost a second!

GSO

Most satellites seem to move across the sky when seen from down here on Earth. But a satellite 22,000mi (about 35,787km) directly above the Equator has an orbit speed that means it goes once around the Earth in 24 hours. The Earth itself spins around once in the same time. So, looking up from the surface of Earth, the satellite seems to hover or hang in the same place all the time. This orbit is called a geostationary, or geosynchronous, orbit (GSO). It means that dish antennas do not have to move or tilt to track the satellite across the sky. They can be left pointing in one direction at it. GSO is used for several types of satellite, especially those which broadcast satellite TV programs into our homes.

SARSAT
Many ships, planes, and vehicles carry a SARSAT radio beacon, or transmitter. In case of trouble or emergency, this sends out radio signals on an emergency channel. The signals are picked up by a world system of SARSATs, Search And Rescue Satellites. The SARSATs send alert signals down to ground stations. The time delay for the radio signals from the emergency transmitter reaching the various SARSATs in their different positions gives the location of the transmitter, and so the search and rescue can begin.

Navigation beacon
A lighthouse sends out pulses of light. The length and pattern of the pulses is a code for the identity of the lighthouse. In the same way a radio beacon sends out radio signals for its own identity or "name," showing ships that it is nearby. The time delay between the radio signals from several beacons allows you to work out your own position in relation to them.

Index